03492

fast
thinking:
appraisal

 **avoid confrontation**

 **agree smart objectives**

 **motivate your staff**

by Richard Templar

contents

fast
thinking:
appraisal

WITHDRAWN

PEARSON EDUCATION LIMITED

Head Office:
Edinburgh Gate
Harlow CM20 2JE
Tel: +44 (0)1279 623623
Fax: +44 (0)1279 431059

London Office:
128 Long Acre
London WC2E 9AN
Tel: +44 (0)20 7447 2000
Fax: +44 (0)20 7240 5771
Website: www.business-minds.com

First published in Great Britain in 2001

The right of Richard Templar to be identified as Author
of this Work has been asserted by him in accordance
with the Copyright, Designs and Patents Act 1988.

ISBN 0 273 65316 4

British Library Cataloguing in Publication Data
A CIP catalogue record for this book can be obtained from the British Library

10 9 8 7 6 5 4 3 2 1

Typeset by Pantek Arts Ltd, Maidstone, Kent.
Printed and bound in Great Britain by Ashford Colour Press, Hampshire

The Publishers' policy is to use paper manufactured from sustainable forests.

introduction

Goodness me, but doesn't time fly. It seems only yesterday that you sent out that appraisal notice. And now the appraisal is due – tomorrow – and you haven't even dug out their file or their appraisal form from last time, let alone sorted out a suitable room.

OK, so maybe you've done all that, but have you got a copy of their job description – yes, an updated one, of course? Have you worked out what you are going to say? Have you identified any training they may need? What about their performance as measured against standards? And surely you've got notes of any critical incidents that have occurred since the last review? No?

Well, in that case, what you need is an express guide to zip you through the appraisal system at breakneck speed and still make sure you end up conducting an appraisal that is useful both to you and the member of your team. You wouldn't dream of going into an appraisal interview with no notes, no job description, no employee personnel file, no nothing, would you? Well, you'd be surprised just how many managers do. But you're going to want to do it fast and smart, right? Then this is the very book for you.

Conducting an appraisal isn't about mulling over how they've been since their last interview or using it as an opportunity to slag them off about all the things they've done wrong. Neither is it an exercise in mutual appreciation. It's a skilled process and one that can do you both good. You wouldn't run your car throughout the year without some routine maintenance, would you? And neither would you let an employee just get on with their job without monitoring their performance – and once monitored they need to be told how they are doing and have a chance to explore that with you in some depth.

I know all this seems a lot to ask when time is so short but it can be done – and easily and efficiently at the same time. Doing something well doesn't necessarily mean doing it slowly – ask a champion racing car driver.

Maybe you've prepared absolutely nothing in which case we are going to have our work cut out – but we can still do it and have you looking pretty cool.

Or maybe you've prepared everything but haven't a clue what you're supposed to say or how to conduct the interview. We'll help you with that as well. You just need:

We are going to have our work cut out – but we can still do it and have you looking pretty cool

tips and shortcuts for getting on top of this interview fast

 guidelines for running a successful appraisal

 speedy information about what to say and how to say it

 checklists to make sure you haven't forgotten anything

… and all presented clearly and logically. And short enough to take in quickly. You've come to the right place.

And what if you've really run out of time and the appraisal interview is scheduled for later this morning? In about one hour? Well, it can still be done – and still done well. At the back of this book, you'll find a brief guide to appraisal interviews in a real hurry. Now that really is thinking at the speed of life.

So chill for a moment and take a deep breath. You may have left everything to the last minute but help is at hand. You're going to have to think fast and think smart but you can do it. Now you know you could do it in 60 minutes if you were really up against the clock, having a whole day seems positively extravagant, doesn't it? OK, let's get started.

key point

APPRAISALS AT THE SPEED OF LIFE

This book will guide you through the seven key stages of appraisal interviews:

1 Before you can proceed you need to identify your objective – what do you intend to achieve by holding this interview and what is the member of staff going to get out of it?

2 Telling the member of staff what is happening. You have to give them some time to prepare and let them know what is expected of them.

3 Get yourself ready. You need certain key documents and you need to have carried out certain key things beforehand – don't worry, we'll tell you what in a moment.

4 Hold the interview. There's a right place and a wrong place. We'll guide you through selecting just the right place and making it appropriate for the interview.

5 Structure the Interview. We'll guide you through such things as setting an agenda – yep, you're going to need one. And setting a time limit, that sort of thing. Essential.

6 What are you going to say? And how are you going to say it? We'll guide you through asking the right questions, making the right noises and displaying the right attitude.

7 How to correct faults and improve performance – constructive criticism.

You may have left everything to the last minute but help is at hand. You're going to have to think fast and think smart but you can do it

fast thinking gambles

So, we can get you through it quickly and smartly but there are risks. If you follow the guidelines in this book you shouldn't go far wrong; you'll conduct a good interview that is worthwhile for both of you, *and* for your organisation. But there is always a risk when you do things as fast as we are going to:

▶ You won't have had enough time to make sure their job description is really up to date – that it matches what they do now as opposed to what they were supposed to do when they first joined your company. These things do have a habit of getting out of sync.

▶ Their personnel file may not be up to date and you simply won't have time to run around collecting all the relevant information.

- You may not have time to find and prepare a suitable room and may have to make do with your own office with all the attendant interruptions and its inherent lack of neutrality.

- You can be so rushed you haven't had time to read their response to the employee preparation document.

- You can even be so rushed you are halfway through interviewing when you realise you have the wrong person entirely – not likely after you've read this book, but it does happen, although only to managers less smart than you.

- Your team member brings a whole lot of points to the interview and you haven't left yourself enough time to work through them.

Fast thinking will get you through the appraisal interview at speed and you'll end up doing a damn good job. And that's the point of the exercise. But for next time you really could do with leaving yourself a little more time. Not only can you do an even better job, but it'll ease the pressure on your heart a bit.

1 your objective

Have you got time for this? The appraisal interview is tomorrow – drawing nearer by the minute – and you're supposed to be worrying about objectives. You just need to talk to a member of your team about their progress, right?

No, not really. You have to do a bit more than just have a chat. You are trying to *appraise* a colleague and that means assessing their performance; evaluating their strengths and weaknesses; reviewing their implementation of company procedures; considering their future and possible training and development needs; valuing their commitment and input – and letting them explain what they need in the way of support, advice, guidance and motivational tools. Whew, bit more than just a chat.

Of course, you could just pull up a chair and have a bit of a chat or tell them off for what you consider they've done wrong, pat them on the back and send them on their way. How do you think they would feel?

You could hold this informal chat in the staff canteen with their colleagues listening in over tea and doughnuts. How do you think they would feel?

You could just summon them with no prior warning – the sort of 'be in my office in ten minutes' routine. Again, how do you think they would feel?

Yep, you could do any of these, but it wouldn't be an appraisal interview. I'm not sure what it would be except not the sort of thing we expect from a smart manager like you.

No, the correct procedure is to think it out beforehand – set an objective if you like. That way the staff will feel that you've taken the time, trouble and effort to really appraise them; that you regard it as important and considerate to give them a proper appointment in a suitably private place free from interruptions and noise; that you consider them worthy of getting your facts straight and that you have bothered to look at their personnel file and know who they are – and what they do.

An appraisal interview is an opportunity to review performance on both sides. They may have a lot to say about how they feel and you really have to set aside long enough for both of you to communicate effectively.

When you conduct proper, well-thought-out and stimulating appraisal interviews your staff feel

REMEMBER YOU OWN APPRAISALS

Cast your mind back over any and all of the appraisals you've had during your working life. Which ones did you consider worthwhile, valid, constructive, helpful? And which ones weren't? Now quickly consider the things you would have liked to have happened and what you consider to be aspects of an inappropriate or badly managed interview.

When you've been on the receiving end of a bad one or a good one it is easy to know what to do to make sure you conduct only good appraisal interviews.

cared about, motivated, encouraged and rewarded. We all like to know how we are doing, to have a set of guidelines against which we can measure our performance.

We like to be challenged to do better and to know when we've messed up. We like our performance to be assessed by people we respect and whose opinion we value. We are all motivated by a desire to please.

So, that's what we are going to do with every one of our appraisal interviews from now on. We are going to use them as an opportunity to:

- ▸ **assess**
- ▸ **consider**
- ▸ **evaluate**

- (▶) review
- (▶) value.

That way our team members are going to feel:

- (▶) cared about
- (▶) encouraged
- (▶) motivated
- (▶) rewarded
- (▶) stimulated.

And they will have a clear view of where they have been and where they are going. That's our objective: *to give our team members documented feedback so they know how they are performing and to let them have an opportunity to discuss how they see their progress and work.*

Now let's see how quickly we can achieve it and what good results it will produce.

for next time

If you haven't taken many appraisal interviews or find them exhausting, daunting, or just plain nerve wracking, make sure you ask for some guidance yourself at *your* next appraisal interview. And ask to go on a proper training course in personnel management.

We like our performance to be assessed by people we respect and whose opinion we value

2 preparing the team member

So the appraisal is tomorrow and your team member is all ready and expectant. They *are* ready, aren't they? You did notify them in advance what was happening and give them the opportunity to prepare themselves? You didn't? Then we have little time and a lot to do. Hang on to your hat – this is staff preparation at the speed of life.

THE OFFICIAL MEMORANDUM

OK, first things first. You have a note in your diary that tomorrow a member of staff is coming for their periodic assessment. Do they know this? Have you informed them? In an ideal world you would have told them at least ten days ago – and told them officially, in writing, in a memorandum.

And the more senior they are the more you would have consulted them to make sure the time and day was mutually convenient. There is nothing worse than trying to give someone an appraisal when they are looking at their watch and fretting about an impending deadline of their own.

THE PRE-APPRAISAL INTERVIEW

For more junior members of staff for whom cover can be arranged easily you can be more managerial in your imposition of a time and day. But if the member of staff is very new you might like to have a pre-appraisal interview. This should only take about ten minutes but is invaluable for them. All you have to do is take them through the procedure and explain what is going to happen. Quick and productive – that's what we like.

The official notification for an assessment should be on official paper and logged and filed so there can be no dispute at a later date about who was supposed to be where. If you haven't already done this you had better do it now – and quickly. It should state:

- ▶ the team member's name
- ▶ their job title
- ▶ the purpose of the memo – their appraisal and the period it covers, i.e. six monthly, annual etc.

There is nothing worse than trying to give someone an appraisal when they are looking at their watch

- ▶ the purpose of the appraisal – to provide feedback on their performance and to give them an opportunity to discuss their work performance and any future training or promotion needs

- ▶ when and where the appraisal is to take place

- ▶ roughly how long it will last – at least an hour

- ▶ who is issuing the memo – yes, I know it's you but give your full name and job title

- ▶ and finally sign it and keep a copy.

Do this now if you didn't at least ten days ago. And attach to it a copy of your organisation's *appraisal preparation document*. What? You haven't got one? Then you'd better draw one up quickly. After all, this appraisal is a two-way process. Not only do you get a chance to discuss your team member's performance but they also get a chance too, you know. And the appraisal preparation document also gives you a chance to see beforehand exactly how they regard their own performance. This could help you enormously if you think they are well below average and they think they are well above. You have a chance to clarify this before the appraisal gets off the ground on the wrong foot if you'll pardon the mixed metaphor.

THE APPRAISAL PREPARATION DOCUMENT

With such a document there used to be a trend to give the employee lots of boxes to tick but that was proved to be unproductive as they merely ticked boxes and you didn't get any feedback at all. Nowadays the current thinking is to give the employee lots of space to fill in their own comments – much better. The sort of thing you might like to provide could look like this.

Name

Job title

Date and time of appraisal

The purpose of this form is to give you an opportunity to prepare for your appraisal so that your assessment can be as productive as possible. Please fill in the spaces as fully as possible.

How do you consider you have carried out the main functions of your job?

Which tasks have you performed best, and why?

Are there any areas of your job which you feel to be unclear?

Do you feel the need for any extra training and, if so, what sort of training would be helpful?

What would be helpful to you in order for you to carry out your job more successfully?

Which aspects of your job interest you the most?

Which aspects interest you least?

Are there any functions of your job which you feel you have underachieved at, and why?

How do you see your future with the company?

If you haven't already issued one of these do it now and give them at least the rest of the day to complete it and get it back to you.

Keep a copy of this form in their file and have it with you at their appraisal of course. And make sure you have read it and fully understand where they are coming from before the assessment.

WHAT THEY CAN EXPECT

By sending out these two bits of paper you inform, reassure and include. Information is essential to any organisation's smooth running. Reassurance is imperative if the staff aren't to be intimidated by the appraisal system – and you certainly don't want that. And inclusion makes them feel as if they belong – which they do.

Their appraisal is important to them. It helps them know *where* they are going and *how* they are doing. Don't let them approach it with a feeling of fear or trepidation. Don't let them feel it means nothing to *you*. Let them know it is a two-way process and be ready to listen. Their appraisal is just that – an appraisal, with the emphasis perhaps on praise. It is not an interview. It is not a school report. It is not a court case. It is not an interrogation. It is an appraisal – an opportunity to *praise* and *raise* issues.

BE POSITIVE

Different organisations have different terminology for this periodic review. It might simply be called an appraisal. But then again it might be a staff development review; a performance review; a development needs assessment; a staff assessment; even a staff development and assessment appraisal. Whatever it is called try to make the staff feel it is friendly, productive and useful. Make sure that when you talk about it you use positive upbeat phrases and don't downgrade it by talking about 'those bloody appraisals I've got to do' – that sort of thing is bad for morale and makes the staff feel you're just going through the motions because you have to. If your heart's not in it, theirs won't be either.

NO SURPRISES

Reassure the team member in advance that there will be no surprises. You aren't suddenly going to launch an attack on them for a past misdemeanour or a lost order or late attendance. You will have dealt with all that at the time. Their appraisal is their opportunity to discuss jointly their performance on a grand scale, their future, their progress, their objectives and focus, their prospects and their approach to the job. It is not a nit-picking session, a telling off or a litany of complaints.

DOCUMENTATION

Make sure you keep copies of every document you send out and receive back, starting with these advance documents:

- ▶ **notification memo**
- ▶ **appraisal preparation document.**

This is protection for your staff as well as for you. If they later claim that you did not mention at their appraisal that you were dissatisfied with their performance but subsequently you have to let them go, how will you justify it if you haven't kept a copy of everything?

for next time

Make sure you get the forms sent out at least ten days in advance. Any new members of staff will need a pre-appraisal interview to let them know what to expect.

When you get their appraisal preparation document back take some time to read it and understand it. Check with colleagues who work closely with the team member if there is a big difference between how you perceive their performance and how they see it.

When you send out the memo informing the team member of the time and place make sure the tone is right – not so formal that it scares them and not so informal that they think they can take it or leave it.

Inclusion makes them feel as if they belong

3 preparing the team leader

Yep, that's you, that is – the team leader. OK, so you've got a date for tomorrow. A member of staff, one of your valued and trusted team people, is coming to see you for their periodic appraisal. You are ready, aren't you? You have gathered together all the relevant documents, haven't you? No? Well then, we'd better be quick. The clock is ticking and there are only so many hours in a day – this day, this one, the one before tomorrow when you have the appraisal to do. Quickly now. Let's run through a checklist of what you need – and why.

First, you need their appraisal preparation document back – and you need to read it. It's pointless them filling it in if you don't. Check it for any major differences. For instance, if you think that a particular aspect of their job is the most vital and interesting and they obviously think it the least important and most boring there is a fundamental assessment gap. You need to check with other supervisory staff to see if it is you or them that has hold of the wrong end of the stick.

thinking smart

PREPARATION IS IMPORTANT

We all like to look flash and think on our feet at times but an appraisal isn't one of those times. You want to be thoroughly prepared. After all a team member is an asset, a useful and productive contributor and an appreciated colleague – surely worth spending some time and effort on. Preparation makes them feel valued and that is important.

THEIR JOB DESCRIPTION

Have you read their personnel file? No? Then go get it quickly and set aside at least half an hour to go through it and see what's there. And what most definitely should be there right at the front is their job description – and it should be up to date, of course. And of course it won't be, will it? It never is. And we don't really expect it to be so. Jobs aren't static and stagnant. They grow organically.

UPDATE JOB DESCRIPTIONS

Every couple of months set aside a little time and quickly check through all your staff members' job descriptions. If you monitor regularly, any changes are easy to spot and quickly put right. If you leave it too long it is a very time-consuming job indeed. A little and often is good maintenance and regular servicing. A long time between services is a breakdown on the motorway.

The only time a job description is bang up to date is the very first day someone starts a new job. After that bits get added on and bits taken away. It happens all the time to all of us.

Trouble with an out-of-date job description is it is very hard to put it to someone that an aspect of their job isn't being carried out effectively if they can turn round and say, 'Well, it isn't part of my job officially anyway – so what's the beef?'

Go through their job description and make notes of any aspects that don't tally with what they actually do. You can then use these notes as part of the appraisal itself. You can check to see if they are happy with any duties that have been added on or unhappy with any that have gone.

The ideal job description

Their job description should be a clear definition of their overall work objectives broken down into key areas of activity. It shouldn't be too long – no more than one A4 sheet – neither should it be too detailed. It should list the key responsibilities, not individual items. It isn't a job breakdown sheet or a list of daily duties. It should be broad in its outlook and cover the focus and objectives of the job rather than the detail or the itemised specifics.

THEIR LAST APPRAISAL

Now you need a copy of their last appraisal. Obviously, if they have joined you since the last reviews you won't have one – but you will still have given them their pre-appraisal interview, won't you?

Hopefully, the last appraisal is completed satisfactorily and there was an action plan. Has it been carried out? If not, why not? If so, was it done effectively, did the team member benefit from it? Did they go on that training course they so desperately wanted? Did they get the extra set of safety guidelines for operating the new ZX4000 they requested? Have they been rewarded/thanked for taking on the responsibility for training the new apprentice? That sort of thing.

Does their personnel file have a critical incident report – the sort of thing that covers major breaches of security or discipline or performance? Their appraisal isn't the place to bring these things up – they should have been dealt with at the appropriate time. That's right, immediately the incident occurred. If they have had a critical incident or any disciplinary hearings then you should be fully aware of them. Have they had any written warnings? Or verbal warnings? (They should have been recorded in writing, yes, I know

thinking smart

CHECKING WITH OTHERS

It never hurts to have a quick chat with other managers who come into contact with your team member just to make sure you haven't missed anything or been too hasty. They may know something you don't or have been aware of a drop in standards that you might have missed. They might also have praise for effort you might have overlooked or it might be outside your area of responsibility. Check also with the team member's immediate supervisor, of course, before their appraisal and make the supervisor feel included in the process.

it's a funny old world.) What about compassionate leave? Any record of medical problems?

Make sure you know this team member as well as they know themselves.

APPRAISAL RECORDS

Naturally, you have a blank one of these, don't you? No? Heavens, we really do have our work cut out. OK, quickly now, we don't have much time. In an ideal world you would start an appraisal with a blank sheet of paper and fill it in according to how the appraisal goes. We don't, however, live in an ideal world and you need some sort of form to give you a structure and a checklist to make sure you've covered everything. If your organisation uses a ready prepared form hopefully it won't be just a case of ticking boxes or giving marks out of ten. You need to write something human and make real comments.

You could draw up something that looks like this.

Present duties

Approach to work

Motivation

Acceptance of responsibilities

Supervisory capacity

Technical knowledge

Planning, organising, co-ordinating abilities

Team qualities

Strengths

Weaknesses

Areas for improvement

Training/guidance/instruction required

Long-term goals

Employee's comments

Manager's comments

Obviously you may have to adjust this to suit your own working environment and organisation but it is a broad outline of the type of thing required. You will notice that there is no space for pay or conditions. These aren't discussed at an appraisal and should be avoided at all costs. Pay should be discussed at a pay review and conditions, benefits and bonuses should all be discussed at another meeting entirely.

That's the paperwork complete. You should have:

- ▶ **job description**
- ▶ **personnel file**
- ▶ **previous appraisal form**
- ▶ **employee's completed appraisal preparation document**
- ▶ **blank appraisal form**
- ▶ **any notes you have made.**

HOW ABOUT YOU?

Good, now how about you? Feeling confident? Nervous? What? It's vital that you approach an appraisal with the right attitude. You're not there to play God, be a judge or jury, be an interrogator or exercise any form of punishment or discipline. You are there to act as a conduit, a catalyst. The object of the game is to try to stay out of the way

AVOID GIVING POINTS

The smart manager knows that by giving points or marks out of ten they generate a feeling, in the team member, of being at school. Much better, and smarter, to make notes and comments in plain English that are easy to read and understand that relate to the job and whether or not it is being done well. Is a B+ better or worse than 6 out of 10? Smarter to say, *'You're doing this part of your job well but I feel it might be more efficient if you always filled in the NZ27 form in triplicate so we all had a copy. What do you think?*

as much as possible and allow the *structure* of the appraisal to take over and run itself. If you are clever you will get the employee to point out their own defects and recommend their own correction or retraining. Lots more about this in Chapter 6 ('What to say and how to say it').

THE JOB, NOT THE PERSON

Now remember you are going to talk about the job – not the person. The job has to be done and this team member has the responsibility to do it. How well they do it is almost irrelevant. What you are interested in is whether the job is being done.

Focus on the job and not the person and you will sail through this appraisal. This especially applies when you are gathering information – especially other people's opinions about the team member. You are interested in how the job is being done, not whether they wear an earring to work or slurp their tea or collect furry gonks on their desk. All these things may make them a colourful person but it doesn't affect how the job is being done.

Concentrating on the job rather than the person makes it easy if you know the person quite well – they may even socialise with you after work – you aren't, in this sense, appraising them but the job instead and whether or not it is being done effectively and efficiently.

If you bear this in mind it makes it so easy to know what topics you can talk about. Lateness, for instance, may be thought of as a topic for an

thinking smart

REPHRASE THE PHRASE

Never say, 'You are inefficient', it just causes alarm, hostility and anger. Try saying, 'The job isn't being done as efficiently as we might expect, what do you think?' Much better, and no reason for the team member to feel threatened or antagonised.

appraisal. Not so. Lateness is a disciplinary matter and should be dealt with at the time it occurs – or a little while after. Same with attitude, interpersonal staff relationships, dress sense or code, sickness, faults, mistakes or slipups.

This is an objective appraisal – not a subjective review. Note the distinction and stick to it. Discuss facts – not opinions, hearsay, rumours, feelings, personalities or prejudices.

Sticking to talking about the job makes it so much easier to correct any problems. You only need explain that certain aspects of the job aren't being fulfilled and the team member doesn't have to be personally criticised. Even the most difficult of employees responds to this approach. Obviously when you are giving praise or credit then you talk about the person rather than the job. It's fine to say, 'Despatch are complaining about late orders, how can we help remedy this? And thanks for helping out last Saturday when we had that rush print job on, well done.'

So, you see, there is no reason to be nervous, in fact your team member is much more likely to be nervous than you are and there's no need to play this any way other than helpfully and constructively.

for next time

Make sure you send out the memo at least ten days in advance, after you have discussed with the employee a mutually agreeable time and day. Send out the appraisal preparation document with it and make sure you specify a day by which it should be returned. Try to make this at least four or five days before the appraisal as this gives you lots of time to study it and make notes. It also gives the team member five or six days to complete it and get it back to you.

For any new staff who are coming up to their first appraisal make sure you have set aside a little time to guide them through the process at a pre-appraisal interview. This doesn't need to be anything more than an informal chat outlining what they are to expect.

Obviously when you are giving praise or credit then you talk about the person rather than the job

4 the appraisal room

Good, we're cracking on at quite a pace now. You've prepared the team member and prepared yourself. All that's left is to decide *where* you are going to hold this appraisal. There are some places where you simply wouldn't ever conduct an appraisal under any circumstances and some situations which are also taboo:

- ▶ **the work canteen**
- ▶ **in a corridor**
- ▶ **in an open-plan office**
- ▶ **in front of colleagues**
- ▶ **at home**
- ▶ **on the shop floor**

- ▶ over the phone
- ▶ via email or fax.

So where are you going to hold it? In your own office? Well, you can but it is not ideal. There are various drawbacks with using your own office:

- ▶ It isn't neutral enough and the team member may feel intimidated – a bit like entering the lion's den.
- ▶ You may find it more difficult staving off interruptions.
- ▶ You, yourself, might be distracted and keep getting up to close the filing cabinet or quickly check a file that was in your pending tray and you suddenly think of a note to add – that sort of thing.
- ▶ The seating arrangements may not be suitable – we'll look at that in a moment.

GETTING TURFED OUT

So where? Well, most organisations keep an interview room for just such purposes. If you don't have one see if you can borrow a colleague's office for an hour or so – they could always use yours. A conference room or even the board room would be suitable at a pinch. You need somewhere quiet, away from interruptions, neutral and with the right sort of seating. You need to know you won't be turfed out unexpectedly or have people poking

There are some places where you simply wouldn't ever conduct an appraisal

their heads round the door every five minutes to see who is using the room.

You need somewhere in which you can create a relaxed informal atmosphere so perhaps the board room isn't ideal. You may not be intimidated but your team member may well be.

LIGHTING

Now lighting. An easily overlooked aspect, but it is very important. Make sure you both have adequate light to see clearly and to be able to make notes. Check any spotlights and make sure they aren't behind you, shining in the team member's face. If they are, angle them away or your staff member will think they are helping the police with their inquiries.

NOISE AND INTERRUPTIONS

Choose a quiet meeting room well away from the hurly-burly of office life. If the builders are in next door don't try and shout above the noise – move rooms. Post a notice on the outside of the door requesting no interruptions and add a finish time on it. Switch off all mobile phones and make sure you're not interrupted by internal phones ringing for you.

Notify any secretarial staff that you are away from your office for (roughly) an hour and that you cannot be disturbed except in a dire emergency – and make sure they know you mean it, this is important. Your team member's appraisal should be very high up your priority list and being interrupted to sign something or to be asked where something is sends out the wrong message to your valued team member.

The key factors to take into consideration when selecting somewhere are:

- confidentiality
- distractions
- furnishing and seating
- light
- peace and quiet.

If you need to book a special interview room make sure you have done so. And make sure you have booked it for long enough – better to over-estimate than be turfed out before you've finished.

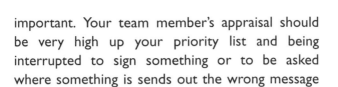

thinkingfast

WHO'S IN CHARGE OF BOOKINGS?

Find out who is in charge of booking meeting rooms and make sure you get on their right side. By winning them over well in advance you often get priority. If you then need a room at short notice they are much more likely to put themselves out to make sure you get one. Don't leave it to the last minute and then find they are on holiday or away from their desk for the morning.

SEATING ARRANGEMENTS

It might be best if you went along now to the interview room and had a quick look to see how the seating arrangements can be adjusted to provide the most informal and comfortable atmosphere.

Traditionally, there are five seating arrangements for such an assessment:

You both sit in low chairs round a coffee table. This is certainly comfortable but impractical for making notes as you have to bend forwards or keep getting up to get files. The table itself may be too small.

You sit at opposite ends of a meeting table. This is good as you can both spread out papers in front of you but it is perhaps slightly too formal and perhaps slightly confrontational.

You sit next to each other at a meeting table. Very good indeed. It is informal, friendly and practical. Ideally, one of you should sit at the short end and the other alongside at the other side. If you sit right next to each other it is harder to maintain eye contact (*very* important) and you have the feeling the other is looking over your shoulder all the time. If you sit opposite each other it is too formal and confrontational.

You sit behind a desk and the team member sits facing you on the other side. Very formal, very confrontational. Avoid it at all costs.

You both sit in office chairs on one side of the desk. Informal but not very comfortable. One of you gets to rest an elbow on the desk but the other has nowhere to spread papers.

So, you've chosen the meeting table and the 'next to each other but at right angles' approach. Good.

REFRESHMENTS

A cup of coffee or tea is always welcome and helps break the ice and settle your team member into the right sort of relaxed approach. Ask them at the start if they would like something and make sure you either have the facilities to make it or can send out for it. Don't offer if you can't provide it or if it is a lot of hassle. You don't need to take a break during the appraisals unless your team member requests it to use the lavatory.

thinking smart

WOOING A CLIENT

Try to create the same sort of atmosphere as you would use to woo a client. This isn't an interrogation or a disciplinary hearing. It is an informal business-style meeting between two colleagues, one of whom happens to be senior to the other.

You can impose the same sort of atmosphere as you would for any other business meeting – since this is what it is – such as jackets off or whatever. You don't need to be all formal and managerial. Relax and enjoy the process yourself – the other person is more likely to as well if you do.

44

for next time

Make sure you have booked the room well in advance. If you are doing a whole series of appraisals make a block booking to cover the lot. Make sure you have notified everyone who needs to know that you are away from your desk and are not to be disturbed. If you allow one petty interruption you open the flood gates. If this has been your style up to now, for next time, make sure you give this job the priority it deserves.

When you have a few minutes to spare, experiment with seating arrangements until you find the right one for you that is relaxed, informal, comfortable and practical,

Your team member's appraisal should be very high up your priority list

5 structuring the appraisal and setting an agenda

You still have some time before tomorrow's deadline and you would be advised to spend a little of it thinking about the structure of the appraisal. Yep, you have to have a structure or you will flounder and lose your way. The structure doesn't have to be too detailed but it has to be there as a framework for building on. The same with an agenda – this can be loose and flexible but you do still need one.

Structure helps the team member have a sense of direction and also provides you with a means of controlling the discussion and making sure all relevant topics are awarded the appropriate time and importance. A structure keeps the thing moving along.

Like any good story an appraisal must have a beginning, a middle and an end.

THE BEGINNING

Take a few minutes to put your team member at ease. Offer them coffee or tea and show them where they can sit and put their papers. Spend a couple of minutes on very light chat just to lighten up the mood and relax you both. Nothing too controversial here. If you know them well you can ask about their children or how that new car they bought is going. Light stuff. Easy stuff. A few pleasantries.

Keep it light

You can keep it entirely to off-work subjects – 'So, how's that new Morgan you bought? Bet it goes like the wind?'

Or you can add in the odd work thing as long as it's light and praiseworthy – nothing heavy – 'So, Robin, I got a phone call about that print design you did and they were very pleased indeed, well done.'

INSIDER INFO

If you know nothing personal about this employee then for
heaven's sake find out something – they like football, they
paint watercolours, they have six children, they used to be
a lifeguard, they once won the lottery – from someone who
works with them. Ask and find out – discreetly, of course.
All you have to do is ask another manager or the team
member's supervisor: 'What does Robin do outside work?'
Then you've got your opening gambit for the appraisal. 'So
I hear you once shared a dressing room with Eric Clapton?
What was that like?'

Signal that the chat is over

> After the chat create an opportunity to signal that
> the chat is over and it's time for the real business of
> the meeting to take place. You know the sort of thing
> – 'Now, let's get down to business', or 'Yes, I'd love
> to see the photographs of your hernia operation, but
> right now we've got an appraisal to do, okay?'

Explain why you're both here

> Then explain why you are both here – 'As you know
> it's your yearly/six-monthly appraisal, Robin.' Then
> explain what is going to happen. 'The reason for this
> meeting is to look at how your job is going [not them,

remember, *the job*] and to see if there is anything you need to help you do it better or improve what you do. We'll have a chat about training opportunities and some long-term plans.' Don't say, 'We'll look at your future' as it implies some doubt as to their security with the organisation.

Point out that you will be taking notes and they should feel free to do likewise. And that any action plans will be decided jointly – you won't impose anything from above.

CREATING AN AGENDA

This is a joint meeting. You may, in theory, be chairing it, but it is still a joint meeting and you have to create an agenda together or they simply won't feel included and involved. You can, of course, lead this creation. Start by saying, 'We need an agenda to decide what points we are going to cover. I thought we could start with a general review of how you see your job and then move on to any specifics you feel need covering. Then I'd like to have a bit of a chat about how the new machines are fitting in and any problems you've encountered. We also need to have a chat about the staffing levels and overtime rates as they've changed dramatically recently. Then we could look at any training you feel you need. And finally we'll talk about long-term plans. How does that sound to you?'

You may, be chairing it, but it is still a joint meeting and you have to create an agenda together or they simply won't feel included and involved

In most cases they'll be only to happy to go along with what you've put to them but they will feel included and involved. If they have items of their own then they can add them to the agenda just so long as they fit into the proper criteria of the appraisal.

Once you've worked out the agenda you can move on.

'Good, so we've got an agenda of sorts, a loose one, but one we can work with, right? Anything else you'd like to add in for discussion?' They may say they want the car parking arrangements added in – it's obviously important to them for some reason so agree and slot it in – it may not be part of their appraisal as such but still worrying them or needing some form of discussion. 'Right, the car parking arrangements. Fine, how about we talk about that after overtime and before training, suit you?' They'll invariably agree.

Good, you're almost at the end of the beginning. All it takes now is an open question to get the ball rolling and the show on the road. 'So, how do you feel the last 12 months/six months have gone then?'

This is an open question – see next chapter for more information on this – but basically it cannot be answered with a simple yes or no and thus invites discussion.

You can of course follow the way the appraisal form is laid out and work through this as an agenda but it can feel a little stilted and formal.

Or you could use the job description as a basis for an agenda but again it might appear to be very formal.

THE BEGINNING OF THE MIDDLE

Ask them to assess their performance since their last review. Then give them your assessment of their performance since the last review. If there is a major difference you need to move straight onto the middle – see next chapter. If you are both in agreement move on to the next section.

thinking smart

PUT YOURSELF IN THEIR SHOES

Before the actual appraisal take a moment or two to put yourself in their shoes. Imagine what their job entails – perhaps you once did it yourself back in the dim past – and what sort of issues are likely to come up. The issues that affect you are not the same ones that are affecting them and the way they do their job. You have to come down a notch or two and envisage what sort of problems they are likely to be encountering. Do this in advance. That way you'll be on their wavelength from the very first moment they enter the meeting room.

You have to create an agenda together or they simply won't feel included and involved

THE MIDDLE

OK, you've opened the batting and got them talking. Now you can talk in some depth about training, the future, any problem areas that have cropped up – we'll look at that in the next chapter in some detail. Just make sure you stick to the point and don't let them wander about or off. Keep the discussion friendly at all times and remember that this is a joint meeting – let them have their say as well.

THE END GAME

Once you've covered all the ground you both want to it is time to wrap it up. There is no point going on any longer than is necessary. As before when you signalled the beginning of the discussion proper, now is the time to signal that it's time to finish.

So you could say, 'Well, that about does it for me, anything else you'd like to add?' Or 'Whew, we've worked through a lot today and I think we've just about covered everything we set out to. Pretty good going, what do you say, shall we call it a day?' Both of these signal that the end is drawing near. And that signalling is very important. It allows the team member to bring up anything else they may want to – and they should be allowed to, of course, just so long as it's relevant – and it brings you to the next phase of the appraisal neatly and effectively.

MAKE CONTACT

When they first come in make a point of shaking their hand and offering them a seat. Of course, you'd do this anyway but make the handshake very warm and friendly. If you don't know how your handshake feels – strong and reassuring or the wet fish one? – get a personal friend to shake hands with you and then ask them to be honest about how it feels. Nothing is more off-putting than the limp, clammy, barely grasped wet fish.

SUMMARISING

Once you've signalled the end you should summarise just so long as there are no further points to deal with. If there are, deal with them and then signal again. Then summarise. You don't have to summarise the whole appraisal – just the action points you have both decided on. You could say, 'So, that's about it. Anything else? No? OK, so you'll improve the credit control system as we discussed and I'll check out those cashier training courses you asked about. And we'll both check back in a week to report on progress.'

Summarising like this is very good for two reasons. It makes sure you – or they – haven't forgotten anything. And it makes sure both of you fully understand what has been decided. They may turn round and say, 'What, I've got to upgrade the computer system? I thought we'd decided Harrison in R & D was going to do it.' Then you can clear up the misunderstanding and summarise again – and move on.

WATCH THEIR REACTION

Watch how the team member reacts when you summarise. If they are not happy about any action plan you've agreed on but aren't saying, they'll reveal their true feelings in the way they sit or fold their arms or sigh or just look blankly at you. (Lots

thinking smart

MAKING NOTES

If you take notes what are you going to do with them? Better to fill in the appraisal form as you go and save a lot of time and effort later having to transcribe your notes and then having to fill in the form. If you do it at the time it's fresh in your mind and you don't forget bits or have trouble deciphering your own handwriting.

more about body language in the next chapter.) If you pick up on such signals don't let it go unchallenged. Say, 'You don't seem entirely happy about having to go on a training course for print buying? What's the problem?' Or 'I thought we'd agreed you'd spend more time on production and less in dispatch and now you seem hesitant to include it in your action plan. Am I missing something?'

Once you've summarised you can move on to actually wrapping up the meeting. This should end on a light and friendly note even if you two might have gone a round or two during it. Remember:

- signal the end
- summarise
- watch for reactions and amend action plan if necessary
- summarise again if required
- thank them for coming
- praise them for their contribution
- end on a pleasantry as you began.

II thinkingfast

So you should say something like, 'Well, that was a good session. I enjoyed that and thank you for coming. Brilliant idea of yours to switch warehouse duties to Rotherham. I'll get onto that straight away. You're doing good work, you know, keep it up. Oh, and wish young Ben luck in his match. That kid's going to play for Chelsea one day, mark my words.'

There, all done – only another five team members to go.

thinking smart

KEEP STAFF – SAVE MONEY

By giving your staff the opportunity to discuss how they feel, as well as providing them with lots of feedback about how well they are doing, you motivate them, make them feel cared about and include them in your team. They feel as if they belong and thus are much less likely to leave. Replacing staff is costly, time-consuming and unproductive. Appraisals help keep staff – and save money in the long run.

for next time

Have a structure worked out in advance including the agenda, even though you let the team member think they are creating it with you. The structure you use can be varied according to the type of employee. For example, some older colleagues may prefer a more formal agenda such as working through their job description or using the appraisal form.

They'll reveal their true feelings in the way they sit

6 what to say and how to say it

Tomorrow is the big day and the clock is still ticking. Yep, tomorrow you have to carry out this appraisal. You have prepared the team member. You have prepared yourself and you have worked out a structure and pencilled in an agenda. That's about it, then? Sorry, but it isn't. What are you going to say? How are you going to say it? How are you going to get this person to really open up and discuss frankly and honestly their performance? What if they clam up and don't want to say anything? What if they turn the tables and begin to criticise you and your management style? What if they burst into tears? What if they are difficult? Or even aggressive?

Yep, you've still got quite a bit to do before you go into the meeting room if you are to handle this effectively and professionally.

You don't have time to learn interview techniques from scratch so what you need now are some practical guidelines to make this appraisal go with a zing. We are thinking – and learning – at the speed of life. Let's cut to the chase.

HOW TO ASK QUESTIONS

You'd have thought it was obvious, wouldn't you? You just ask. So let's try it:

'How's the job going?'

'Fine.'

'Any problems?'

'Nope.'

'Well, that's that then. Thank you for coming.'

 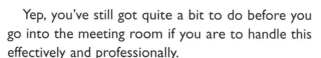

thinking smart

WE NOT I

You will find your team member much more responsive at their appraisal if you talk of 'we' rather than 'I'. 'We need to look at this problem area,' rather than 'I think there's a problem here.' That way they will feel much more involved, and that it is a discussion rather than a telling-off process.

OPEN AND CLOSED QUESTIONS

See, it just doesn't work. You've asked *closed* questions – ones which allow the team member to give a one- or two-word answer. And this means they don't open up, don't discuss, don't enter into the spirit of the thing. And that usually means very short, ineffectual appraisals which benefit no one, least of all the team member. It is only fair to them for you to put a little bit more effort into it and ask *open* questions – ones which require more than a one- or two-word response. Let's try it again:

'*So how do you feel the job's been going since the last appraisal?*'

'Oh, not too bad, but I have had problems with integrating the new software.'

'*Why is that?*'

'Because the matrix doesn't mesh with the ZX4000 programs as we were promised. It makes us very slow completing our returns which means dispatch get held up. That causes all sorts of problems as Jackson simply hates delay and I've had to work a lot of overtime which has meant ...'

And so on. See the difference?

Quick recap:

- ▶ **Closed questions allow one- or two-word answers.**
- ▶ **Open questions require a fuller answer.**

Closed questions are this sort:

- ▶ **Have you met your targets?**
- ▶ **Are you happy with this part of your job?**
- ▶ **Are you concerned about the staff turnover in your department?**
- ▶ **How long did it take to get up and running again after the fire?**

Try these again as open questions and see if the response is different:

- ▶ **What do you think about the targets you were set for this year?**
- ▶ **Which parts of your job are you happiest with?**
- ▶ **Why are you losing so many staff?**
- ▶ **What was the biggest challenge in getting up and running again after the fire?**

Ask open questions – ones which require more than a one- or two-word response

HAVING THE TABLES TURNED

It can happen at an appraisal – you get the tables turned on you and suddenly you are under attack for your managerial style or a complaint about the way you handle things. Be calm. Stay calm. Don't be defensive. Regard this as an opportunity to open up the discussion. Ask the team member for specific examples of what they are talking about. Listen to them and repeat back what they say. If they've brought it up it is because it means something. Look for a solution together.

OPENING UP A DISCUSSION

Open questions not only indicate that you are genuinely interested in the answers but they also offer an invitation to the team member to unburden themselves and open up. Open questions open a discussion; closed questions close it down. For instance, closed:

'How's your new trainee getting on?'

'Fine.'

Open:

'How are you finding the new trainee?'

'Not bad, they seem very keen. I would like them to have a bit more practice on the rolling excavator machine but I simply can't spare them from the loading bay at the moment. I really could do with another pair of hands there if we want them to get some more experience. Do you think it would be worthwhile if we …?'

DISCUSSIONS AND FACTS

Obviously if you want to find out facts you need to ask closed questions. You don't ask open questions if you want figures, dates or percentages. But often asking a closed question first will demand an open question afterwards to get the discussion rolling:

'How many staff do you need then for the packing department?'

'Seven.'

'Why so many?'

'Because four of them are needed to actually do the packing but then we have to have someone to drive the lorry and at least two to shift the pallets from stores. Actually, I could really do with eight but I don't think the budget could stretch to that, could it?'

And as they've asked you a closed question you can safely answer *'no'*.

BODY LANGUAGE

You don't need to watch individual gestures – arms folded, legs crossed, sullen face, head dropped, shoulders sagged – to know when you are not getting a positive response. Watch instead for clusters of gestures. Two or three or more indicate a resistant team member. Notice and ask why they are unhappy about what is being discussed. Don't leave it and hope they will perk up. Be aware that whatever their body language you will unconsciously 'mirror' it – copy it. You can't help this unless you consciously fight it and make sure you are open and upbeat in your own body language, otherwise you get a downward spiral.

OTHER TYPES OF QUESTIONS

Open and closed questions aren't the only ones you can ask. Depending on what sort of response you want you have to vary the way you ask things. And there are certain types of questions you really don't want to use – ever.

Searching closed

This is where you need specific information to establish a definite point from which you can then lead the discussion.

'So how many copies can you collate now with the new machine?'

'Fifteen hundred an hour if only we could get it running properly.'

'And how is that affecting your delivery times for the Newman contact?'

Searching open

If you want specific information but also want the discussion to open up then you ask a searching open question:

'And then exactly what happened after you reversed over the MD's dog?'

Or:

'So you shut down the machine and cut the power, but what happened to the boy's arm?'

Empathetic questions

Use this sort of question when there is an emotional content to what the team member is saying. They offer a sympathetic compassionate approach which might be appropriate.

'And you are so upset about being transferred to the printing department that you are considering leaving?'

Or:

'So how did you feel when the client stormed out?'

Empathetic questions often include a measure of repeating back to the employee what they have just said to you – or at least repeating back the emotional content. Try not to put any interpretation on the emotional side such as:

> 'Don't you think being so upset about being transferred that you'd consider leaving is a bit silly?'

Or:

> 'Surely you realised it was your own fault the client stormed out?'

If an emotional issue like this is raised then there is a reason behind it – your team member genuinely feels something. Ask about feelings. You might think them silly – but think it only. Their feelings are real and to be taken seriously. You can't deny them the right to have the feelings and it is your job to allow them to express them.

thinkingfast

TAKING NOTES

There is nothing more off-putting than someone taking down what you say verbatim. If you aren't filling in the appraisal form but just taking notes keep these to a minimum. Fast managers don't take notes but fill in the appraisal form as they go. If it ain't on the form you don't need it. Your notes are for you but this is a joint process. They may wonder what happens to the notes later or what you are writing. Be open and fill in the form as you go and get their assent on every category.

'What if' questions

These take the form of asking the team member to imagine a scenario or put themselves into another's position or to get them to think about a new idea or situation. They can be very useful in getting a discussion going or getting the employee to consider their responsibilities in a new light.

They shouldn't ever be derogatory:

'What if we all behaved like that?'

Or:

'What if we all wrote our own job descriptions – wouldn't get much done then, would we?'

Rather, try getting the team member to see things from someone else's point of view:

'What if you'd been in charge that day, what would you have done?'

Or:

'What do you suppose would have happened if that order had fallen through?'

You're not apportioning blame or telling them you think it is their fault that something bad happened, merely getting them to see the consequences of their actions or the repercussions throughout the organisation.

'What if' questions don't have to begin 'what if'. You can also ask:

- ▶ **What do you suppose ...?**
- ▶ **What would you do if ...?**
- ▶ **How would you have handled ...?**

'What if' questions ought to contain a word such as 'if', 'suppose' or 'imagine', however, to make sure the team member realises that it is a hypothetical question and not one which is likely to happen immediately. There's no point saying:

> *'What if you were in my shoes, what would you do with an employee like you?'*

They simply don't have the experience to answer such a question and it only makes them feel and look small. So don't do it.

thinking smart

NO 'BUTS'

Never finish praising a member of staff at an appraisal – or any other time – with the word 'but'. Once they spot you do this it destroys any future praise as they know what's coming:

> *'That was a very good presentation, but ...'*

> *'I liked the way you handled that client, but ...'*

The same goes for 'however', 'although', ' nevertheless' and 'yet'. You will find that saying *'it might be worth bearing in mind'* is more helpful if you want to make a point and sharpen their performance.

Leading questions

These can be useful if you want to set an agenda or formulate a structure that they feel part of but which you are actually not giving them too much choice in. The downside of them is that the team member may feel they are being led — they may agree but not *feel* in agreement. This can lead to resentment or regret later.

Leading questions may be useful for agendas but not for committed action plans.

You can say:

'So we'll discuss the job description first and then specific problems if that's all right with you?'

But not:

'Bet you really regret doing that now, don't you?'

They may agree but not feel any regret at all and you have lost a valuable opportunity to find out how they really feel.

'Alternative close' questions

I'm sure you know this is a very useful sales technique but it also works if you are trying to get a team member to agree to an action plan. Basically, you give them a choice and they feel they have to go down one of the two routes you have put to them. Clever, eh? Not only that — it also gives them a feeling of control. It's *their* choice:

'So do you want to switch to print or design after Christmas?'

'Would you like to go on this training course now or leave it until next month?'

'Do you think you can patch things up with Sam or do you want me to have a word?'

The alternative close questions are good when you really do want them to take some action but feel that if you left it to them they might not do anything. It also works with children – *'Do you want to have one more swing then go home or a quick go on the roundabout before getting back into the car?'*

Rapid fire questions

Do not use this technique unless you are a police officer or a member of a foreign interrogation squad. Rapid fire questions are exactly that – fired so fast that the person simply doesn't have' a chance to answer any of them. It confuses them and disorientates them. But there are some managers who do try to use this technique at appraisals so they can get the whole thing over with as quickly as possible. Pointless. You know the sort of thing I'm sure:

'So you think you're doing OK? But what about that incident in production last week? Bet you think I've forgotten those lost delivery notes? Well, I haven't

Not useful and not to be used.

WORD THE QUESTIONS CAREFULLY

Good, so word your questions carefully. Take your time to think about *how* you are going to ask, as well as *what* you are going to ask. Any of the techniques just examined can be used in an

thinking smart

DON'T TALK DOWN TO THE TEAM MEMBER

They may be a lot younger and less experienced than you but don't talk down to them. Avoid using jargon that they might not understand. Avoid foreign phrases – '*laissez-faire*', '*Schadenfreude*', '*sine qua non*' – that sort of thing. Don't use high-falutin' managerial speak. No acronyms that they may not be familiar with such as GIGO (garbage in, garbage out) or RDB (regional development board). If they don't know what you are talking about chances are they won't ask for fear of being seen as uneducated or stupid.

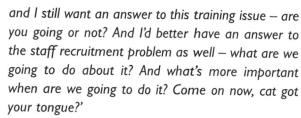

inappropriate way as well as a beneficial one. For instance, you could use the 'alternative close' question to elicit a response that might be quite wrong and not what the team member wants to say at all:

'So do you feel you're doing OK or do you need a bit more training?'

What hope has the employee got? They have to answer that they're doing fine or submit to a training programme that they may not want or need. What if they *aren't* doing fine but don't feel the need for any training? Do they need some other support instead? What if they think they're doing fine and still feel they want some additional training?

Better to ask:

'Do you feel you are doing OK?' or *'How do you feel you are doing?'*

And wait for an answer before going on to suggest training or whatever – your response depends on their answer.

Make sure you give them space to answer, that you haven't filled in the blanks for them. Try not to phrase questions so that the answer is already implicit in the question such as:

'I suppose you reacted that way because you felt inexperienced, didn't you?'

This is a leading question gone wrong – leading them to a place they might not want to go. Better to ask:

'Why do you think you reacted that way?'

LISTENING

An important skill for any manager to learn. I'm sure you are very good at this or you wouldn't be the smart manager you are:

- ▶ Good listening lets the team member take some time before they speak. You don't have to jump in and break the silence.

- ▶ Good listening allows each question to be answered fully without interrupting.

- ▶ Good listening means listening and not taking notes at the same time.

thinking fast

SUGGESTIONS NOT PROPOSALS

If you want their agreement quickly and without fuss try suggesting rather than proposing. A suggestion begins *'shall we …?'* A proposal begins with *'I think we should …'*

Suggestions are easy and quick to go along with. Proposals are sort of imposed and you may get resistance which slows the process down.

Make sure you give them space to answer, that you haven't filled in the blanks for them

Good listening means using appropriate phrases to encourage the employee to carry on such as 'go on', 'yes', 'I'm listening', 'take your time', tell it in your own words', 'there's no rush', 'good' and so on. Even just making the odd noise will encourage them to continue and prove you're not asleep.

So, I guess we've pretty well exhausted questioning in a brief sort of way. This stuff can be studied for years and I guess all you need is this quickest of guidelines to get you through this appraisal tomorrow – or do you need some training?

 thinking smart

GOOD LISTENING SKILLS

If you want to show that you are listening and paying attention to what is being said try looking interested – lean your head slightly forward and to one side as if you were hearing intently.

Ask questions to show you are listening.

Repeat back what has just been said to you: *'So if I've got this right, you want to …'*

Bring the discussion back on track – this really shows you're listening.

for next time

Make sure you have worked out which questions you need to ask – and the way you are going to ask them – in advance.

Good listening allows each question to be answered fully

7 constructive criticism

We all need it but can we all take it and can we all dish it out? Many managers feel distinctly uncomfortable with appraisals because they don't like criticising their team members. However, failure to take the bull by the horns, so to speak, leads to a lot more problems than constructive criticism ever does.

DEVELOPING YOUR TEAM

A lot of managers fail to criticise staff properly whom they know to be 'difficult'. And, of course, if they know a team member is pretty easy going they may well criticise more than is necessary. The result is that the person who needs it the most gets it the least and the one who needs it least gets the most. Very unfair indeed. And all because the manager felt intimidated by or fearful of the process of proper constructive criticism.

And if you don't carry out a proper constructive critical stage in the development of your team then how can you expect them to improve? It is the manager's right to criticise. Without criticism poor performance will continue and any opportunities to improve will have been squandered. It's OK to criticise at an assessment — your team are expecting it.

WHEN TO CRITICISE

Criticism is best done at the time it is most needed — immediately. What we are concerned with here, of course, is criticism at an appraisal. But the rules of good constructive criticism apply in all circumstances anyway. If you are storing up criticism for the appraisal you are storing up trouble. A lot of managers do, but it is an unsavoury practice. Better to do it as soon as you spot something that needs correcting. Also criticism is often a bit of a shock to the employee. They didn't realise that what they were doing was wrong or not being done according to company procedures, or even just plain daft.

STOCKPILING CRITICISM

And remember what we said early on — no surprises at their appraisal. So you can't just suddenly turn round at the appraisal and produce a list of faults and begin criticising. It just won't do. You should have dealt with these things at the time – not stockpiled them like some picky squirrel. How would you feel if your boss did it to you?

STORING UP RESENTMENT

The other problem with storing criticism is you are also storing resentment. If the team member does something wrong and you fail to take corrective action immediately, chances are that by the time their appraisal rolls around they will have done it another 20 times. And what has that done to your temper? Chances are you will find out at the appraisal when all that resentment boils over and there is trouble with a capital ubble.

thinking smart

CRITICISM SANDWICHES

A lot of managers use the criticism sandwich technique. It isn't a good one. This is where they sandwich the criticism between two bits of praise. They hope it will make the criticism a bit more palatable. It doesn't. It merely harms the praise. Better to be bold and upfront about it. Get the criticism over and done with and then have two praise puddings instead. Much tastier.

Criticism + storage = resentment
Resentment + appraisal = trouble

Criticising is correcting a fault. That's it. It isn't:

- nit-picking
- complaining
- deliberately finding fault
- being on their back
- looking for trouble
- moaning
- carping
- being finicky
- being hypercritical
- showing disapproval
- being fussy.

Criticism is correcting a fault. You do it pleasantly, politely, graciously, even. You spot a fault and you put it right. If the same fault is carried out often you need to look at retraining. If errors continue it might be a disciplinary matter and that's not criticising. Criticising is something done to correct a fault at the time. It's no good having a team member coming into an appraisal and you launching into a list of things that need correcting if you've never said anything before. *No surprises.*

YOU CAN'T EXPECT PERFECTION IMMEDIATELY

Or even eventually come to that. If a team member is going off track in a lot of areas you can't put them all right at the same time. Better to concentrate on one or two key areas first. Get them right and then tackle another couple of problems. None of us can take an infinite amount of criticism. Ration it a bit and take your time. You are building a productive team member here so don't expect miracles overnight. Invest in time and work it through in stages.

CRITICISM AND PRAISE

If criticism is correcting a fault, what is it when no faults need correcting? That's right, praise. And praise and criticism should go hand in hand. It is part of your job to notice when a task is being carried out well – and offer praise. But it is just as much part of your job to notice – and correct – any faults that are occurring. The smart manager doesn't just dish out praise but also gets the staff used to being criticised so they expect a degree of fairness. If they do something wrong they expect to be told and corrected. And obviously when they do something well they expect it to be noticed – and praised.

SO WHAT'S AN APPRAISAL FOR?

If you can't store up criticism for the appraisal you might wonder what it's for. Simple. It is to review progress. It isn't a correcting session where you go over old ground and try to put everything right. It is an opportunity to review why things go wrong in the first place. It is a chance for both of you to discuss what the team member needs in the way of support or training or encouragement or motivation to make sure faults don't occur in the future. It most certainly isn't a moaning session where you berate the member of staff for all their past errors.

thinking smart

THE WIN–WIN SITUATION

Don't let the team member go away after the appraisal thinking it was all one-sided. You need to concede ground, give a little, as well. If you want them to go on a training course and they seem reluctant you can always offer a trade: *'Look, you go on this course and I'll make sure Andy deals with your paperwork while you're away so you don't have too much to come back to.'* Or: *'You work the overtime we need and I'll make sure you get the extra days off you want next month.'* That sort of thing. This way you both come out feeling you have achieved a result.

The smart manager doesn't just dish out praise but also gets the staff used to being criticised

CONSTRUCTIVE CRITICISM

If you do have to criticise a member of staff – at the time of the incident – then it should be constructive. This means you point out the fault – and then offer ways and means of doing it better, doing it properly and doing it again if necessary. Constructive criticism is just that – constructive. You are constructing a better way of doing it. Merely pointing out a fault is useless if you don't offer an alternative at the same time. The objective of criticism should always be to improve performance and create better working relationships. If your criticism doesn't work towards this goal then it isn't criticism but one of those listed earlier.

CRITICISM BASED ON FACT

All too often a manager will steam in and blow their top when something has gone wrong. This rather quaint and old-fashioned style of management is thankfully dying out. But there are still those among us who do it. All criticism should be based on fact. Find out:

- ▶ **who did it**
- ▶ **why it was done**
- ▶ **what they thought they were doing**
- ▶ **what they thought they were supposed to be doing**
- ▶ **whose responsibility it was**

- ▶ what can be done about it now

- ▶ what's to stop it happening again.

The same goes for appraisal. It's no good discussing something with a member of staff unless you are really sure of your facts:

'So, your job description says you are responsible for the production of the annual show brochures but we don't seem to have had any for the last year. What do you think is going wrong here?'

'Well, the annual show was cancelled last year so no brochures were needed.'

'Oh, was it?'

Don't you look foolish now?

thinking smart

OFFERING AN ALTERNATIVE

Don't criticise if you can't think of a better way of doing things yourself. There isn't much point saying to a team member, *'Your presentation wasn't too effective because the overhead projector failed twice at crucial points'* when you both know the projector is defective and you have no plans for replacing it. You have to offer an alternative way of doing things – a better way – or you run the risk of the team member turning round and saying, *'Well, what should I do then?'* and then you'll be lost for words and have to mumble and slink away. Be prepared before you say anything.

Be sure of your facts – and have evidence

Always be sure of your facts for the appraisal – and any time you need to criticise a team member. You may be challenged so you'd better be sure of yourself. This means having the evidence. It doesn't mean snooping or playing detective. It doesn't mean collecting a police-type dossier on employees. It just means being accurate and having details of faults. You need to know when and how and where – that sort of thing. Otherwise:

> *'Ah Robin, I need to talk to you about all this lateness of yours. We need to do something about it, don't we?'*
> 'What lateness?'
> *'Well, you have been late quite often recently.'*
> 'When have I been late? Name a single day when I've been late.'
> *'Um, well, er, I'm sure you have been.'*
> 'Well, I haven't.'
> *'OK then, off you go.'*

Much better to have the facts at your fingertips:

> *'Ah Robin, I see you were late on Monday and Tuesday of last week and again on Wednesday and Thursday of this week. What are we going to do about it?'*

So have your facts to hand and the evidence collected. But before you talk to the team member you need to:

- ▶ **test the evidence**
- ▶ **substantiate the facts.**

Corroborate and discuss

Never criticise anything unless you have first checked with another member of staff that you've not been sold a dummy. It does happen and you need to both protect yourself from possible recriminations and the member of staff from false accusations. Never launch a critical attack. Always ask first:

'So, Sam, you've lost the Madison contract. Well, I'm not happy and we need to take some firm action to stop this sort of thing happening again.'

No, no, no. Try instead:

'So, Sam, what's happening with the Madison contract?'

'Ah, the Madison contract is being phased out, but a new one, and one much more in our favour is being drawn up now.'

'Good work, Sam'.

Of course, it might not have been *quite* so easy:

'So, Sam, what's happening with the Madison contract?'

'Ah, I think I've blown it.'

'Do you want to explain that?'

'Well, I thought I was pushing hard but it seems

too hard. Madison didn't like being called a stingy badger and walked out. I'm sorry.'

'So let's look at where you think you've gone wrong and then we'll look at ways of making sure it shouldn't happen again. Suit you?'

'Thanks.'

A BLANK SHEET OF PAPER

Every appraisal should start with a mental blank sheet of paper. If you had to criticise staff during the period between appraisals then that is old stuff. It has been dealt with unless it's a recurring problem and then, as you know, it's retraining or disciplinary. Once you've criticised a team member and they have corrected the fault satisfactorily then move on and cover new ground. It doesn't even need mentioning at the appraisal if it has been successfully rectified. Nothing is worse for an employee than having all their misdemeanours dragged up at an appraisal. The body should have been buried, there is no need to pick over the bones. It is a spent conviction.

BRINGING UP PROBLEM AREAS AT AN APPRAISAL

Their appraisal is a chance to discuss how they have been doing their job. Not criticising doesn't mean you can't bring up problem areas – but they should be discussed. A discussion is quite different from criticising. You begin by asking them how they see things. Then perhaps point out that the organisation might need more or better and then formulate an action plan. At no point have you criticised the team member. You are reviewing the job, remember, and how effectively it is being done. Criticism is a personal thing. An appraisal is an objective review.

BE SPECIFIC

Bringing up problem areas at an appraisal is easy if you approach it correctly. It isn't criticism but a chance for the team member to focus on specific things that may need improving:

'So how are you finding the new ZX4000 machine?'
'Pretty good although it isn't as reliable as the old ZX3000.'
'Why is that, do you think?'
'Well, it has a tendency to recalibrate the steel rollers automatically when I've manually set them.'
'But doesn't it say in the manual that they have to be set automatically?'
'Does it?'
'I think you'll find it does. From my experience the ZX4000 is the bee's knees when it comes to reliability but you do need to follow the instructions pretty

closely. It's much more complex than the old ZX3000 and you can't assume the operation is the same.'

'Oh, I thought it was identical.'

'Not at all. Do you think a quick refresher course might be useful?'

'Not 'arf. That would help a lot.'

Now you know they needed some retraining. You knew they weren't reading the manual properly. In fact, you knew their approach was lazy and lax. But did you need to say that? Did you attack them? Were you critical? Nope. But you've got the result you wanted, they feel good about themselves and they think you helpful and that your managerial style is rather friendly and effective. What's more, you've revealed your experience and they know they can't try to pull the wool over your eyes in the future. Good work.

JOINT ACTION PLANS

When you tackle problem areas at an appraisal always try to find a joint solution. Trying to impose a solution from on high is ineffective and rather pointless. The team member simply won't respond well if you try this approach. If you get their co-operation and involvement they are much more likely to stick to an action plan – after all, it's their baby too.

BEING A CHOREOGRAPHER

If you use all the techniques in this book to get the team member to open up and discuss things you may create an atmosphere that is both relaxed and informal. And sometimes it can get too relaxed, too informal. The discussion can turn into a general chat about goodness-knows-what. You have to see your role as a choreographer – directing the dance and keeping everyone in step, including yourself. Even managers can get distracted. You are there to participate but you are also the manager and have overall control. Any divergences have to be turned back quickly and politely: *'That's brilliant, Robin, I didn't know you knew so much about early nineteenth-century porcelain but we do need to get on and work our way through this agenda. Let's get back to the appraisal, shall we?'*

Why an action plan?

Even top people need plans to stretch them and improve their skills and give them more training. An action plan is always welcome as it gives you and the team member a result. It gives them something to report back about to fellow team members and a sense of achieving something concrete. An action plan may be no more than a simple note of chasing up an order or telephoning

If you get their co-operation and involvement they are much more likely to stick to an action plan

a supplier and checking problems have cleared – for example, a review in four weeks to check there are no more problems with the ZX4000.

It might be a training course, a refresher course, a new responsibility, a transfer to a new department, increased duties, lessened duties, a new project, some hands-on experience of new technology. It might even be some guidance towards promotion.

It is only fair to give your team members all the help they need to carry out their role to the very best of their ability. After all you get lots of help. You've got this book.

WRAPPING IT UP

Make sure you summarise everything you've discussed and that you have both agreed the action plan. If you want them to sign their appraisal form get them to do it now. After that it's just a question of finishing on an upbeat note. Thank them for coming. Shake their hand and open the door for them. Again thank them and pass a pleasantry similar to the one you gave them when they arrived – 'And don't forget to wish Ben luck from me.' Or: 'Let me know how the bungee jump goes.' That sort of thing. Then they leave. You remove everything from the meeting room that you brought with you

and go get yourself a well-deserved cup of coffee.
Well done.

DEALING WITH DIFFICULT PEOPLE

No matter how hard you try and how good you are at your job there will be times when you encounter difficult people at appraisals. These are the ones who seem intent on making your job as challenging as possible. Whatever you do you must not rise to the bait. Count to ten (under your breath, of course), practise a simple relaxation technique such as deep breathing, leave the room for a moment or two if it gets really heated. And if the worst comes to the worst you are quite within your rights to cancel the appraisal and reschedule it for another time. But do try to see these people as a challenge rather than as a difficulty – that way you'll think of ways and means of dealing effectively and productively with them rather than getting irritated.

FOLLOWING UP

If you two have agreed an action plan then make sure you *both* follow it up. Don't just expect them to achieve results – you need to monitor them. You need to make sure that they know that you have their best interests at heart and are prepared to remember the action plan and work on it as much as they have to. You have to do what you have said

It is only fair to give your team members all the help they need

you will do. So if you promised to look out those training manuals make sure you do. If you said you would check on a possible transfer to your Ipswich branch for them make sure you do.

Build in dates by which things have to be done or some form of monitoring results. That way you can make notes in your diary when you get back to the office and keep an eye on the situation.

Work out well in advance what you are going to say and how you are going to say it.

Make sure that any mistakes that are being committed have been criticised at the appropriate time and not saved up for the appraisal.

Practise asking open and closed questions and see the different responses you get.

Work out in advance solutions to any problem areas that you need to discuss – that way you won't be caught on the hop when they ask what they should do about it.

Build in dates by which things have to be done or some form of monitoring results

appraisal in an hour

If you really are up against it and only have an hour to prepare you have to think on your feet and act quickly – this is appraisal preparation at the speed of life. And it is preparation in an hour – not an appraisal in an hour, that takes as long as it takes:

- ▸ **You probably haven't got time to check their job description (see pages 27–29) beyond making sure that they are still doing the job they are supposed to be and that they haven't been transferred to another department entirely or even promoted.**

- ▸ **If they've completed and returned their employee appraisal preparation form (see pages 21–23) read it now, quickly. Use a highlighter to mark anything that you think you will need to discuss or focus on specifically.**

- ▸ **Make sure you've got their personnel file. You might not have time to read it in depth now but do open it at least and make sure you know who you are talking to.**